SECRETS TO BECOMING AN EFFECTIVE PUBLIC SPEAKER

Copyright © 2019 Jim Kokocki

ISBN 979-8-643-26240-4

Printed in Canada.

SECRETS TO BECOMING AN EFFECTIVE PUBLIC SPEAKER:

A Common Sense Guide to Effective Public Speaking

JIM KOKOCKI

TABLE OF CONTENTS

HOW TO USE THIS BOOK

I have been practicing and refining my speaking skills for more than 30 years. I joined Toastmasters in 1987 and served as International President for the organization from 2015-2016. Toastmasters International is a communication and leadership development organization that operates more than 16,000 clubs in more than 145 countries. The not-for-profit organization was established in 1924 and remains strong today. Toastmasters has played a significant role in my development as a speaker and leader.

My desire for you, the reader, is to see the role that knowledge, practice, and feedback serve in your development as a speaker, and to use the material in this book to discover, fully understand,

and effectively communicate all that you have to say.

Acknowledgements

There are many people to thank for helping me to put these ideas on paper. I thank my editor, Joanne MacMillan, for her guidance and her attention to detail. I also want to thank my good friend and fellow Toastmaster Dave Stonehouse for his keen eye and his professionalism in applying his public relations sensibilities when providing feedback to this work.

I also thank the many Toastmasters around the world who offered feedback as I practiced and refined these ideas, and to my mother and sister for their encouragement and support over the years.

INTRODUCTION

Communication skills always rank high in the skills employers wish to see in prospective employees. I have been applying attention and effort to improving my communication and leadership skills for more than 30 years. When I began my career I was a very shy computer programmer with strong technical skills, but lacked the skills and confidence to express my ideas in any group setting. I was encouraged to join Toastmasters so in 1987 I joined Toastmasters in Saint John, New Brunswick, and in 2015-2016 I had the honor of serving as International President and Chair of the Board of Directors for the global organization. That experience saw me speak to audiences as large as 3,000 people, and travel to more than a dozen countries, including South Africa, Zimbabwe,

Australia, Japan, Vietnam, the United States, and the Czech Republic.

Toastmasters operates a network of clubs around the world where people visit, join and become members, usually for about $200 USD per year. Each member works through structured learning programs to craft speeches and then deliver them at club meetings. Once the speeches are delivered, oral and written feedback are provided on areas where the speaker performed well and perspectives are offered on areas for improvement. Additionally, members become involved in the mechanics of planning and managing each Toastmaster meeting enabling further skill development.

I am often asked how to become a better public speaker. In my experience, if someone wants to be a great public speaker, they need:

1. some knowledge of the skills and techniques of public speaking,

2. regular practice of the skill and techniques, and

3. feedback that enables improvement.

I'll explain why each is required.

1. KNOWLEDGE

Speakers need to understand the techniques of public speaking. If you want to be a strong speaker you must observe others, continue to study, and acquire information related to the skill. At a minimum, your knowledge must include how to assess the needs and expectations of your audience, how to organize your speech, how to use stories to make your speech memorable, and how to use eye contact, gestures, and purposeful body movement to effectively deliver your speech.

2. PRACTICE

Public speaking is a skill. Skills require practice to keep them sharp. Consider the top athletes in the world. These athletes practice basic skills on a regular basis, whether that involves free throws, batting practice, skating drills, or putting. Skills require practice. Public speaking is a skill and skills require practice.

3. FEEDBACK

Finally, speakers require feedback on their strengths and opportunities for improvement. Strengths should be emphasized, and weaknesses should be corrected or minimized. Feedback is best delivered by coaches, mentors, and supportive peers. Friends and family are usually too supportive to offer objective developmental feedback.

MORE ABOUT PUBLIC SPEAKING KNOWLEDGE

There are a number of sources to help you build your knowledge of public speaking. Books, one-day courses, online videos, TED Talks, university courses, and blogs provide content to help you build knowledge.

Content related to public speaking knowledge includes the following areas:

Organizational Techniques

There is no communication if the message is not received and understood. To be received and understood, your message must be organized effectively.

Your approach will vary based on your audience and your purpose in speaking. For example, if your purpose is to entertain an audience your material needs to emphasize drama, witty comments and humor to maximize your impact. Such a presentation needs to be carefully organized and planned to build to some surprises and some laughter, although you can humor and entertain an audience without generating a lot of laughter.

Most of my experience is with business presentations where the audience wants to quickly know the purpose of my talk. Purpose could be to share findings, to make a decision, to present a point of view on an upcoming decision, or to offer an update on an initiative.

A familiar business structure is *"tell 'em what you'll tell 'em, tell 'em, and tell 'em what you told them."* I used to think this was demeaning to the audience. It isn't.

In our busy world people are distracted. They may be physically present for your presentation but not fully mentally present, thinking about their last meeting, their next meeting, a sick parent, a child nervous about a test at school or unfinished tasks. By clearly using this structure, you improve the chances that your audience will get at least some of your message, and you demonstrate that you are organized and respectful in how you will use your time with them. Tell the audience why you are in front of them, then take them through the details, and end by offering a simple summary.

My favorite structure is past-present-future. This structure can be used to develop a major presentation or to answer simple questions, especially the questions that catch you off-guard.

Here's an example of past-present-future in a situation that helped me during a spur of the moment interview. One day, I walked into the City Market in Saint John. I saw a TV cameraman and a reporter with a microphone. I tried to avoid eye contact but they approached me and asked, "What are your thoughts on the upcoming vote by city council to spend $20 million on a new police station?"

I don't like expressing political opinions publicly but I calculated how I could answer this safely with a past-present-future structure. My response was something like, "Well a few weeks ago, a neighboring community voted to spend a similar amount on an arena for use by many of their citizens. I hope with their vote tonight, council considers how to spend our money for the best use of all citizens." The answer was a little evasive, but accurately reflected my opinion and it was well received. I didn't express a strong opinion, but it was organized and it was used in the news clip.

A well-practiced, familiar structure such as past-present-future can be a lifesaver when organizing short or long talks. You look organized because you are organized. You've imposed structure on your response.

Assessing the Needs and Expectations of Your Audience

Before you begin planning your speech, make an assessment of your audience's knowledge related to your topic. If you assume your audience has little exposure to your topic, and instead they do, you will annoy or bore them with basic details and background.

If you assume your audience has good exposure to your topic and they have little, you'll talk over their heads.

One way to assess knowledge is with personal contact. It's likely someone has invited you to speak on your topic. This person is a stakeholder who wants your presentation to be well received. Speak with this person and ask her, "How familiar is the audience with the topic?" It may be difficult for the person to say precisely but she can provide a general outline.

During this conversation, ask for the names and numbers of a couple of key people who want your presentation to be successful. Contact them and let them know what you've learned about the familiarity level. Ask if they have a different point of view. You might also ask them what they would see as a successful outcome from your presentation. This may uncover more insight. For example, perhaps your presentation sets the stage for changes or decisions the group will undertake soon.

Second, if you haven't received good guidance on knowledge level, you can ask the audience directly about their familiarity level. Simply ask "Who is new to this topic? Has anyone had some exposure?" and adjust based on the mix in the room. Respect the minorities, but speak to the majority.

How to Use Stories

Stories make presentations memorable if the story leads to a point. Many cultures use stories to teach. Consider Confucius in Chinese culture, or Grimms' Fables, such as *The Tortoise and the Hare.*

Find relevant stories and practice telling versions of them with friends. Tell short versions, longer versions, and change the sequence of elements within the stories to discover how to get the best impact. If you're speaking to a business audience, conversations you have with leaders in the business while you're preparing your presentation can uncover relevant stories from within the organization. Ask for permission to share the stories with your audience, as these should have high relevance to the group.

FINDING STORIES

Stories are all around us. For a speaker, the skill required is documenting the story and recognizing its lesson or purpose. There may be multiple lessons or purposes embedded in one story.

I like to carry around a four-by-six inch booklet that fits conveniently in a jacket pocket. I always have several on the go. I use them to capture notes, ideas, and stories.

I recommend making note of any story you tell to a friend or colleague with any degree of passion. It might be funny, or dramatic, or a simple customer service experience, good or bad.

Here's an example: A few years ago, I was on a flight from Toronto to Edmonton. Typically, when I get seated I quickly scan the entertainment offered in flight to see if there is any music I want to listen to or any movies I want to watch.

On this flight, my screen wasn't working. I called one of the attendants over and he said he had to reset all of the screens because only about 20 per cent of the screens were working. As I looked around, I could see that for each set of three seats it seemed one was working. So maybe more than 20 per cent, but certainly not an acceptable level of service.

The attendant reset the system and still my screen didn't work. A different set of screens around me seemed to be working but mine wasn't. So the attendant announced the screens would be reset again.

Once again, only a small portion of the screens came to life and mine wasn't one. So I sat back unconcerned because I had some material to read and some work to do.

But then I heard a conversation in the row behind me. A male passenger was complaining that his screen wasn't working. The flight attendant said, "Yes sir, your screen won't work today, but you'll get a coupon."

What?! He was getting a coupon! If he was getting a coupon, I should get a coupon. I didn't know what the coupon was for, but I wanted a coupon. So I called the flight attendant over.

I didn't want to simply blurt out that I wanted a coupon. I didn't want to appear crass. So I said,

"My screen isn't working." He said, "yes we reset the system twice and the screens just aren't going to work reliably today." I just looked at him because I wanted to hear him say, "you're going to get a coupon."

He saw me kind of staring at him so he said, "the system is like a big computer, and the computer won't work today." There was a pause. I finally said, "Will I get a coupon?"

"Yes sir, everyone on the flight will get a coupon."

This is a silly little story. But it's a good example of poor communication, and overly long communication. I could have simply said, "I heard passengers will receive coupons because the screens aren't working. Is that correct?" I've also used this story to discuss customer service, changing expectations, and on being clear and simple in expressing your needs and desires.

I hope you see that the trick is to recognize funny or dramatic stories that we tell with passion, and capture them for later use.

Stories are assets. There is great art in telling our stories. The art includes discovering them, recognizing them, understanding their value, seeing the point that is illustrated, knowing how to maximize the impact of the story, and having the confidence and skill to dramatize or exaggerate some elements of the story for maximum impact.

Eye Contact

A great speaker has a way of looking at the audience in such a way that each member feels at some point that she made direct eye contact. Eye contact engages the audience.

Additionally, eye contact helps the speaker to assess whether his presentation has been understood. Ideally, you're looking for heads nodding as the audience agrees with your points. If members of the audience aren't receiving your message, you'll see some wrinkled brows or heads being scratched and you can make the effort to restate and clarify.

While eye contact and assessing audience response is very valuable, a speaker also needs

to understand that some audiences simply aren't responsive. Some will be quiet and reserved but still get value and enjoyment from your presentation.

Gestures and Purposeful Body Movement

If you're speaking to entertain, you will likely want to use some dramatic, even over-the-top, gestures to support your message. But even if you're delivering a formal business presentation, some gestures are appropriate. When you gesture, your voice will usually modulate and break from monotonous tone. Simple gestures include using your hands to count, raising and lowering your arms, or purposeful movement around the stage.

More About Practice

Public speaking is a skill. Skills require practice. There are many ways that you can practice your public speaking skills.

I usually construct my speeches in eight-to-ten minute segments, and continue to break these into two-to-three minute segments. For example, a segment could be a customer service story, or a description of a situation in the past that has caused an organization be in a predicament.

Organizing in small segments serves many purposes including enabling me to rehearse these small components when I have just a few moments, for example when I'm driving somewhere, or exercising.

PRACTICE BEFORE AN AUDIENCE

When you're ready to exercise your skill in front of people, you'll need to find an audience. Here are some options.

Service clubs

Service organizations such as Lions Clubs, Kiwanis, and Rotary Clubs often have people speak on topics of general interest to their membership. I'm aware of presenters who have talked about their travels, their industries, and their non-profit organizations. Make a call to one of these organizations and ask who books their speakers. Ask if they'd be interested in having you on their program. You may end up booked weeks in advance. If you're flexible, you may benefit from an earlier speaking slot if another speaker cancels.

These opportunities are usually unpaid but provide you an opportunity to deliver a message that has value to an audience, and to practice interacting with an audience.

Volunteer Leadership

There are many volunteer boards and committees that need assistance and perspective to effectively fulfill their mission. Enter these commitments only if you can commit to service for at least two years, and attend meetings and events regularly.

As boards and committees work towards their mission, there is ample opportunity to broadly practice the communication skills of listening, speaking, crafting your responses and contributions, and speaking persuasively. There may even be opportunities to speak publicly to represent the committee or the board.

TOASTMASTERS INTERNATIONAL

I am a long-term member of Toastmasters International. Toastmasters' mission is to empower individuals to become more effective communicators and leaders. The organization is comprised of thousands of clubs around the world where members join and support one another practicing and refining communication and leadership skills as each progresses individually within the structured learning program.

A Toastmasters club will provide you with opportunity to plan and deliver speeches on topics you wish to explore, and to receive written and verbal feedback from other participants.

TED Talks

TED Talks have become popular events for sharing ideas. An industry has been built around these talks in coaching and mentoring speakers.

Guest Lectures

Often universities, high schools and other learning institutions will invite people with expertise to speak to their classes. In my experience, the best way to uncover these opportunities is to establish your credibility on a topic, and work with your network of contacts.

MORE ABOUT FEEDBACK

Feedback is vital to a speaker's development because we can't learn in a vacuum. Other people can see things that we are unable to see. We all have blind spots.

You've likely watched and listened to speakers with habits such as playing with change in a pocket, flicking of hair, frequently adjusting a tie, playing with glasses or jewelry, starting every sentence with the word "so'" or using a great deal of filler words like "um," and "ah." Any of these habits are fine if they're not distracting. If any are done too frequently, audience members will find it difficult to focus on your message.

No speaker wants to distract from her message, however, we're usually unaware of how we may undermine our message. Thankfully, there are ways to fix this.

HIRE A COACH

Find someone you're comfortable with who can assess your performance and offer constructive feedback. Coaches can help with focusing your topic, organizing your speeches, practicing your speeches, finding speaking opportunities and, of course, assessing your performance as a speaker. You'll need to determine in which areas you desire coaching, and the budget you have available for coaching services.

Find a Mentor

A mentor is similar to a coach in that you are drawing from their experience and wisdom to improve an aspect of your performance. A mentoring relationship can be formal or informal.

A formal relationship is when it is acknowledged that the mentor possesses skills and experience you admire and you agree to work together to develop your abilities. An informal relationship is when a mentor simply engages with you to understand your goals and offers to provide feedback.

Toastmasters International

Toastmaster clubs provide excellent environments for speakers to present and receive feedback and perspective from a variety of attendees with differing backgrounds. And members receive periodic training on how to deliver strong, effective, and constructive feedback.

In my experience, some of the best feedback I've received was from people who were unfamiliar with my topic. Specifically, terms or concepts which I might assume to be familiar to my audience, sometimes are not.

VIDEO RECORDING

You may choose to have your presentation professionally recorded. The group to which you are presenting may typically record presenters with your permission. That can be a bonus for you to see yourself from an audience perspective, and perhaps to use the video content to market your speaking talent.

You might also ask a friend to sit in the audience and record some, or all, of your presentation. If you do, I recommend asking the friend to move to various parts of the room so you'll get different perspectives which might reveal strengths or opportunities for better voice projection, or eye contact and audience engagement.

Watching yourself on video initially is usually difficult. You'll likely be surprised by how your voice sounds. Other people are fine with the sound of your voice, but you may be surprised. You may notice repetitive gestures and habits. If this is the case, don't be concerned. If you are surprised or disappointed, it only means you have high expectations for yourself and that's very good. You likely delivered a fine presentation to an audience who had modest expectations, although you may have failed to exceed your own expectations.

Longer Presentations

I've noted previously that past-present-future is an effective organizational technique. In most of my speeches, I aim to present a series of eight-to-ten minute components. Eight-to-ten minutes is my sweet spot in which I can generally speak about two or three concepts.

Because I've become comfortable with this personal rule of thumb, longer speeches simply become a series of shorter speeches. For example, a 40-minute presentation becomes four shorter presentations organized to flow together.

Even within this model, for a 40 minute speech, past-present-future can be embedded into the entire presentation. I might start the speech by describing how I arrived at a current issue (past), describe current efforts to address the issue (present), and the majority of the speech describing how we can move forward (future), and importantly the audience can take action.

PowerPoint and Other Presentation Tools

There is ample advice available in books and videos on using slides in presentations. My personal approach is to always assume some aspect of the technology will fail. This means I will be able to present my content without it.

If you adopt this philosophy, slides become merely a guide for the key points in your speech. Often a visual or a video can help set the stage for your topic. If the technology does fail, your ability to still deliver will amaze and delight many audiences. So I advise to make light use of Powerpoint, Keynote, Prezi, and similar products, and to simply use slides to introduce segments of your presentation.

Do not use a lot of text on your slides. Slides aren't designed to be read by your audience, or to be read by you to your audience. Slides should only introduce and support your key points.

Perfectionism

When it comes to delivering presentations, perfectionism holds people back. Sometimes people feel they don't have enough facts and research, and that they'll be challenged on their material. At some point, you will be challenged on your material, and a little later in this section I will advise how to respond.

First, recognize that you have something important to say. Prepare a plan for delivering your speech, and find a group you can deliver it to. Joining a Toastmasters club and participating will provide you opportunities to plan, to deliver, and to receive feedback on how your message was received.

You'll learn that the presentation you plan is usually not precisely what you deliver. A presentation is an interaction with an audience. Ideally, you let them know what the purpose of your talk is, what you hope to accomplish with the speech, and you proceed receiving smiles, nods and other indications that your message is being received.

Please don't let perfectionism hold you back. You have something important to say. Get experience in planning, and delivering the message in front of people.

When Your Knowledge is Challenged

When you present, someone may challenge your facts, your knowledge or your opinion. However, the facts you've researched are the facts you have discovered. You've worked to acquire your knowledge and you've formed your opinion based on fact, knowledge and your experiences.

If you are challenged by an audience member let him state his case very briefly, thank him for sharing his point of view, and then invite him to speak with you after the conclusion of your speech to share further. When you invite him to share put a boundary in place. For example, you could say "I'm interested, please share your point in 60 seconds before I continue with my presentation."

Remember, you are the presenter invited to speak and share your knowledge, experience and observations. Reiterate with confidence what your research uncovered, and deliver it to your audience. You have something to say, the audience wants to hear your message. Respect an individual with another point of view, but stick with your plan, and deliver for your audience.

Meet Your Audience at their Energy Level

Your engagement with the audience begins well before you say your first word. Sometimes your audience is reserved, and sometimes enthusiastic. I invite you to view Barack Obama's speech to the Democratic National Convention in Boston in 2004. It's available from a few sources when you search, "From the Archives: Watch Obama's 2004 Speech at DNC."

Notice how he engages with the audience before the speech even begins. He projects confidence, and quiet enthusiasm.

You may have observed presentations when the audience was reserved and a speaker comes out with high energy and enthusiasm. This usually doesn't work. It's better to meet the audience at the energy level they exhibit and bring them on a journey. If you want them to be excited by your ideas you need to take them on a journey where they hear and experience your excitement about your ideas.

Use of Quotes and Jokes

Some people advise that a presentation needs some humor, and therefore to start with a joke. I believe humor is important in most presentations. You've likely heard humor in eulogies, but such humor is usually based on personal experiences with the person who has left this world.

I am not a proponent of using jokes or quotes unless they have a message that ties directly to your key points. I've heard of new presenters spending too much time researching jokes and quotes they assume will entertain the audience. In my opinion, the best humor comes from our personal stories and experiences. When we share our experience, it makes us more relatable.

While some will advise you to open with a joke, my advice is to simply acknowledge the event, or someone you chatted with before you took the stage, or someone who made the event possible. This enables you to connect with the people in the audience and display some appreciation with at least one of the members.

If you are nervous and you open with a joke, and if the joke falls flat, your confidence will drop, and the audience's confidence in your presentation will drop.

Use a joke or quote only if there's a clear point that bridges to your main topic. For example, if you're speaking about organizational change you could effectively employ this quote attributed to Woodrow Wilson:

"If you want to make enemies, try to change something."

If using this quote and the audience only offers polite laughter, you can show confidence in your material by acknowledging the polite laughter, and moving into your points about change.

MANAGING FEAR
AND ANXIETY

Many people fear speaking before an audience. Virtually every speaker feels anxiety before he takes the stage. It's good to feel anxious because that means you care and you want to do well. In the world of sports, many athletes are physically ill before important games but once the game begins, the skills they've developed and practiced kick in and they perform. Ideally, your speaking experiences will be similar in that you will feel anxiety, although I hope you don't get physically ill. In my experience, you will find that once you take the stage, the skills you've developed and practiced carry you through.

Sometimes people fear public speaking because they are nervous about the audience reaction. Don't worry, audiences want the speaker to perform well. In your experiences as an audience member, I'm sure you never wanted to see someone bomb, or to be boring. So be confident in the fact that the audience wants you to do well.

The Event: Before You Speak

If you've ever arrived early before a major sporting event, you may have noticed one or more athletes relaxing on the bench, or even sitting in the stands. Sometimes they're visualizing how they'll approach the game. Sometimes they're simply soaking in the environment and getting some familiarity with the venue before the action starts.

This is relevant to speakers as well, and it is part of my preparation routine. It's valuable to arrive early, walk the stage or speaking platform, visualize your audience, and test any microphones or other audio-visual equipment you will be using.

There may be a microphone available at your venue. There are several types of microphones. I suggest if the venue has a microphone, you should use it. There is a reason they've determined they require a mic. You may be confident your voice will project, but if the venue has invested in a microphone, the operators know that the room is dead, or swallows up sound.

My preferred mic is a lavalier that clips on a lapel on a jacket, or connects with an unobtrusive headset. This type of microphone has a clip-on transmitter that usually goes onto a belt, and most AV professionals will run the wiring inside and up the jacket, with the wiring reappearing at the lapel. If you're working with a pro, simply stand with your arms outstretched like you would at airport security, and let him or her position the microphone so it will stay in place during your presentation.

I like the lavalier mic as I typically wear a suit or jacket when I'm presenting. If you're not wearing a jacket you need to give consideration to how such a microphone may clip on to your attire. It's good to have a belt. It's good to have a lapel. A t-shirt or similar attire can make it difficult to find a good location, and it could be very awkward to place the mic.

When wearing such a mic you need to be aware of your movements and gestures. If you thump your chest and there's a mic on your lapel, there may be a loud blast delivered to your attendees.

Handheld microphones are also common. While these are designed to be portable, you might find that it's fixed mounted to a lectern. You will want to know that before you step onstage to address your audience.

If you're using a handheld microphone you should practice with it before your speech, but generally you will want to hold the microphone a little more than a thumbs length from your mouth. You will want the microphone positioned at this distance quite consistently, so you'll need to avoid excessive movement of your hand.

When your speech begins there's no need to pronounce a cliched 'testing, testing, 1-2-3.' That's fine during rehearsal. Instead when you take the stage offer a simple 'thank you, thank you' with a pause of a few seconds, and repeat this procedure a couple of times. This will indicate you appreciate any applause, and allows a sound technician to hear the volume and make any adjustments.

It is critical for my confidence that before I speak that I know I've been on the stage, that I've visualized my audience, that I've had at least a couple of minutes experience with the mic and AV equipment, and that I've met and been friendly with the AV person. This is all about minimizing surprises, and establishing solid working relationships.

Take the time to arrive early and reduce surprises. Imagine arriving at the last minute. You're introduced but your name is mispronounced. You step onstage and see a handheld mic mounted at the lectern. You strive confidently to the lectern, and grab the mic before you move to the center of the stage But you discover the mic is fixed in place. You fumble with the mic, to see if it is in fact portable but just stuck in place. You give up and decide you'll need to work from behind the lectern. You offer a big "how's everybody' into the microphone and the sound reverberates around the room surprising the audience and you. Not a good start.

This is not a far-fetched scenario. Arrive early, and minimize the chance that you'll be surprised.

BEFORE YOU SPEAK — AN EXAMPLE WITH 3,000 PEOPLE

I'll offer an example when I had to prepare for a major presentation. In 2014, Toastmasters International held our annual convention at the Kuala Lumpur Convention Center in Malaysia. One of my responsibilities was the host our World Championship of Public Speaking in the 3,000 seat Plenary Hall.

For these sorts of events I was provided with a script. I had read the script several times, understood where I might take a significant pause and noted those areas with a colored marker and the word 'pause.'

I'd also removed some minor text I didn't want to use, and added a couple of phrases so the presentation would be true to me and my style. I'll note that there are times you absolutely need to stick to prepared script, for example, if the material is possibly controversial. However, most times you'll want to add some brief comments to show your personality and engage with the audience.

In order to warm up the audience and attempt to get a laugh I decided to insert a phrase in Mandarin, as we were in Asia and a significant proportion in the audience had Mandarin as their primary language. I certainly did not.

One of the phrases in the script was 'please do not take photos during the presentations.' We were having a speech contest and we never want a speaker to be surprised and blinded by the flash from a camera or a phone. I had talked with some friends who are fluent in Mandarin on how to say the phrase and based on their comments I had written in my script phonetically 'boo kah pie jow,' which I was told translated to 'no photos.'

The event was to start at 9:00 am so I arrived at 8:00 am and walked the stage. There was a handheld microphone set in place on the lectern, and it was easy to remove. I adjusted the position of the mic while mounted so it worked for my height, and tested the sound with the AV professionals.

I placed my script on the lectern and made sure I could read the print. The font size was fine, and it was easily readable.

I had printed the script single sided because I didn't want to be flipping pages during the presentation. I had had the script stapled together but then removed the staple, so I could slide the page I would finish to my left, and expose the second page, and so on. Sliding the pages is less noisy as you're not rattling pages as you flip them over.

The stage was setup with a lectern on the front left, and a chair for me about ten feet behind the lectern. During the main part of the program I would introduce each presenter, then move back and sit unobtrusively behind the lectern while she delivered her presentation, after which point I would rise, shake the presenters hand, and then return to the lectern to introduce the next speaker.

Once I had scanned my script, and looked over the room from my position at the lectern, it was still early so I sat in my chair and watched the early birds file into the three-thousand seat theater. A few people involved in the production and setup passed by and I chatted with some of them.

By 8:45 am the room was mostly full and again I walked around the stage, feeling very comfortable in the environment, and then stepped backstage to be ready for the 9:00 am start, when I would be announced and step out from behind the curtains.

My point in describing my preparation on that day is to help you the reader to envision how you can prepare for any significant event with which you're involved. In my case, I did not want to step onto the stage for the first time and see 3,000 people and freeze in any way.

My time spent on the stage at 8:00 am minimized that risk. I had invested time and energy early in the morning to acclimatize to the environment and to be ready.

And if you're wondering, my attempt at Mandarin did garner some laughs, most likely due to my poor pronunciation.

THE BASIC LEADERSHIP SPEECH & THE VALUE OF REPETITION

Some leaders struggle with planning and delivering talks to their teams. And some teams and leaders struggle to achieve expected results. Part of the reason results aren't achieved is because teams and people don't understand organizational goals and don't understand overall strategy and direction, let alone how their activities and efforts can support success.

To boost the likelihood of success, it's critical that leaders be effective at explaining, and repeating, strategy, direction and goals, the very what and why of an organizations' path to success. Further to this it is critical that it is made clear what behaviors and actions employees can take that will enable success and are likely to be recognized by senior leaders.

A basic leadership speech structure sees the leader explain, or reiterate, overall goals, indicate progress, recognize the behavior of people or teams who are contributing to results, and describe how people and teams can contribute to overall company success.

To make the structure of a basic leadership speech clear;

1. Explain, or reiterate, strategy and goals

2. Indicate progress towards goals

3. Recognize examples of behavior by people or teams that will lead to overall success

4. Describe how all employees can support behavior leading to success

To illustrate, let's imagine that a leader delivers a speech to her team once each quarter. In the first quarter, the leader should spend much time acknowledging the successes of the previous year, and then move onto the strategy and goals for the current year. As this is the first quarter in our example, this is the time to go into depth on what goals were selected, the process that illustrates why they were selected, perhaps even what goals or directions were deferred and why so. Some employees will want to understand this quite fully and all should understand them generally.

Next the leader can indicate progress that has been made to reaching the goals. Early in the year this may be minimal and perhaps there's been no progress at all. In that case, it becomes all the more important to recognize people or team behavior that will help make progress towards achieving the goals. For example, a sales team may have scheduled meetings or demonstrations with some new clients. Such behavior is worth recognizing, because others will see what gets recognized, and repeat the behavior. Finally, to describe how others can contribute to overall success, the leader can simply indicate how the behavior relates to overall goals and encourage all employees to support the behavior.

In quarter two, the leader can remind the team of the overall goals, but not delve in why these were selected. By quarter two, some progress will have been achieved and that should be made clear to all. Now again, individual or team behavior that results in overall success should be recognized, with a call to encourage all employees to support the behavior in their day-to-day efforts.

The same structure can be used in quarters three and four. You'll note there is repetition in the structure, and in the content. In quarter one, the content is heavier on strategy, and that shifts as the year progresses to more emphasis on results.

In this example, it is helpful for the audience to be familiar with the structure, and to hear strategy repeated, because sometimes it takes time and repetition for a message to be received.

At times a leader can make the mistake of thinking that because she told a team once, or twice, about strategy, that they all understand this. There's a great study and exercise known as 'The Tapper Study' conducted in 1990 by Elizabeth Newton, a graduate student at Stanford University. In the exercise, one person is assigned to be a tapper is asked to tap out the words to a familiar song like Happy Birthday. While the song is tapped out, one or two people serve as guessers, and are asked to listen to the rhythm of the words being tapped out and guess the name of the song. This sounds easy to people, but it's not, and there's a leadership lesson that becomes clear during the exercise.

During the exercise, the tapper and the audience will know the name of the song, but the guessers will not. I often conduct this exercise in my presentations, and when I conduct it, I have the guessers seated with their backs to a screen. On the screen I project five or six song titles that the tapper and the audience can see. To engage the audience, I will usually ask them to show by applause how many would like to have each song tapped, and progress through the list to find the most popular choices to the audience members. To be clear I'll ask 'who wants to hear song number 1,' and then 'who wants to hear song number 2' and so on. But then I'll thank them for their input, indicate the choice is entirely at the discretion of the tapper, and then ask the tapper the number of the song he chose. Obviously, it's important that the title not be revealed, because we want the guessers to listen and identify the title based on the performance of the tapper.

With the scenario set and understood, the tapper and the audience know the title of the song about to be tapped. The guessers obviously do not know the title of the song. Then the tapper proceeds to tap out the words of the song. It's important he does not do drum fills or other identifying noises. If you're familiar with the song We Will Rock You by the band Queen, you'll know there are some clear opening hand claps that would make it easy to guess. This exercise is about tapping words only.

During the exercise, usually the guessers are unsuccessful. (However, in my experience very familiar songs like some Christmas carols and songs like Happy Birthday are sometimes recognized and guessed.) When I conduct the exercise in my seminars, I like to use songs from Elton John, Abba, Elvis or familiar television themes like the Brady Bunch or Friends. I will note that I ask for participants that are roughly my age and who are familiar with songs from the 80s and 90s.

As the tapper progresses with the song, there are usually nods and smiles of familiarity from the audience, and puzzled looks from the guessers. I've had some tappers who weren't very skilled at tapping out the words, but in that case we still need to progress with the exercise.

Why are the guessers usually unable to identify the song based on the words being tapped? Well, the audience is aware of the title and all the context the title enables. The audience benefits and suffers from what the Stanford study author Newton terms the 'curse of knowledge,' because the audience members know the title, and they are able to quickly identify the rhythm of the words and acknowledge them. The people with the knowledge hear the tapping sounds and are able to mentally organize the rhythms with the lyrics with which they are familiar. But the guessers are searching to organize, to find meaning or structure. They usually fail to find clues that help them organize the tapping rhythm.

The leadership lesson is that, in a similar manner, a new employee sitting in an audience where a leader is speaking about unfamiliar business metrics, will struggle to understand the significance of the message. That employee will similarly be looking for clues to help him organize and make sense of what he is hearing.

Newton's study indicates that the people who know the title in advance can 'hear the song in their heads.' As leaders, when we speak of goals, objectives, progress and metrics, we need to work to ensure that team members understand strategy and direction, that they can hear that 'song' in their heads.

Leadership and communication are closely linked. Great leaders communicate in a manner that enables others to understand direction and how their behaviour and contributions impact organizational success. As a leader you will want to do all that you can to ensure that all stakeholders can 'hear the song in their head.' This usually requires some repetition of strategy and goals.

To provide a method to assist in making clear strategy, goals and progress, I reiterate the structure of the basic leadership speech;

1. Explain, or reiterate, strategy and goals

2. Indicate progress towards goals

3. Recognize examples of behavior by people or teams that will lead to overall success

4. Describe how all employees can support behavior leading to success

Example – Two speeches and Audience Engagement

I write this in March 2020. A coronavirus COVID-19 has thus far caused 4,300 deaths worldwide. 66,000 people have overcome and survived the virus, however sporting events and other public gatherings are being cancelled. It's a serious situation for all of us as worldwide we work to contain the rapid spread of the virus.

It's a timely and relevant topic, so I decided to deliver a speech at my Toastmasters club about good habits that individuals can practice to avoid acquiring or spreading the virus. The speech was delivered to the group before we entered the phase of social distancing or physical distancing that has been used to limit the spread of the virus.

As it turned out another attendee decided to deliver a speech on the same topic, and this provides me with an opportunity to illustrate two approaches to the same material.

The other speaker is beginning his speaking career and his approach was to offer lots of information about the COVID-19 virus. This included where it seems to have originated and how it has spread now to many countries, with lots of statistics on infection rates and mortality rates, tips on avoiding the virus, and more. It was a good speech containing lots of facts. This type of speech appeals to the head, to logic.

My plan had been to make it more personal and practical for the audience. One of the provisions for reducing the spread of the virus was to avoid touching the face, as the eyes, nose and mouth are gateways for bacteria and the virus to enter the body. I had twenty minutes before my speaking slot would arrive, so during that time I noted the name of everyone in the room, and quietly tallied every time each touched his or her face, in order to inform them during my speech and make a point about how we need to change our habits. I was surprised because only one of the twenty attendees did not touch his face, and two attendees touched their face more than twenty times in the twenty minutes.

As the prior speaker had covered some of my material, I needed to adapt my material. I had noted some areas where I could elaborate if I had additional time and that planning proved very helpful.

When the section of my speech came to reveal that I had been recording how often each person touched his or her face, I let them know that I had been doing so. I said that 'yes, I'm that guy,' as I was a little concerned that some might take offense, although none did. Based on the positive response in the room, I continued and asked each to estimate how often each had done so, and I was surprised by the level of self-awareness.

My point in relating this story is to show that by envisioning your performance, you can introduce an exercise or experiment to make the material more personal and relevant to each attendee. Additionally, it is worthwhile to understand how you might adjust your remarks if a previous speaker, or your introducer, covers a significant portion of your material.

SPEECH ANALYSIS – DONALD TRUMP JULY 21, 2016

When I served as a senior elected leader in Toastmasters International, there were quite a number of media engagements. This one was quite interesting.

I served as International President of Toastmasters from August 2015 until August 2016. On Wednesday, July 20, 2016 I received a call from Dennis, one of our public relations professionals. He said we had an interesting PR opportunity available. The Los Angeles Times had requested that we write Toastmasters style speech evaluations of the acceptance speeches

from the two candidates who were being nominated to run for President of the United States by the Republican and Democratic parties. He continued by saying that the first speech was the next evening, Thursday, by the nominee for the Republican Party, Donald Trump.

I replied with absolute silence, because Trump was, and remains, a controversial figure as a result of comments he has made, and because of tweets he has sent.

Dennis heard my silence and quickly responded with 'no, no, this will be good for us. We're not commenting on policies or positions, we're only evaluating and commenting on his speaking style and overall approach.'

I understood and agreed to the request. I had known that the speech was occurring on Thursday, but I didn't expect to be listening, analyzing, and writing about it.

Dennis was glad I agreed and then indicated that I would need to submit the evaluation within a couple of hours after it's completion, so that it could be published in a timely manner. There would be two evaluations from Toastmasters International, one from me, the International President at the time, and one from our most recent winner of the World Championship of Public Speaking, Mohammed Qahtani, from Saudi Arabia.

On the Thursday evening, I watched the speech online with some note paper in front of me. I listed some typical areas to assess and wrote them on my page so I could categorize my observations. The list included organizational structure, gestures, vocal variety, eye contact, and segment transitions. As I listened, I jotted notes indicating key points and transitions so I could later analyze the flow and see how one part of the speech led to another.

Once the speech was completed I reviewed my notes, analyzed the delivery and prepared my commentary. Once I was satisfied, I submitted it to the Times. Here's what I sent them.

Donald Trump acceptance speech

I'm pleased to offer some comments and observations on Donald trump's speaking style I observed during his acceptance speech of the Republican nomination on July 21, 2016. Trump is clearly a skilled communicator and I offer these comments from my perspective.

I observed several strengths such as simple, clear word choice and quite good use of vocal variety. Specifically, at times he spoke in a quiet and sincere manner and more frequently with passion and more volume. His pacing during the speech was very good and varied. At times he spoke rapidly and at times more measured. His use of eye contact was strong looking with purpose throughout the auditorium while he spoke. Use of gestures and body language was limited with an over reliance on the "ok" gesture and pointing. Simply having his hands in an open position would add variety and would appear very natural.

I'll add some general comments. At one point the speaker clapped into the microphone which is typically very loud. When in front of a microphone it is better to make a clapping gesture without actually clapping one's hands together as the audience will see the gesture and follow.

Trump is very good at calling attention to key points by interjecting phrases such as 'Think of this! Think of this!" Additionally, he was very good at reading the audience energy and allowing the audience to express their enthusiasm. There were a couple of misses in this regard. When he was introduced there was loud applause and cheering and Trump did a good job of letting the crowd express themselves. But then he started with a quiet, low key 'thank you, thank you." This was an opportunity to comment on their enthusiasm and let them express their excitement further. Generally, a speaker should try to meet the audience at their excitement and energy level.

There was some opportunity for more consistency of his message. I noted at the start an emphasis on working with the audience on a message of 'we are a team.' However later in the speech he spoke of 'my opponent.' "We' became 'my.' This seemed like an opportunity to further unite the crowd with 'our opponent.'

All in all, Trump is a talented speaker and during his seventy-minute address displayed very strong speaking skills.

SPEECH ANALYSIS – HILARY CLINTON JULY 28, 2016

After analyzing Trump's acceptance speech, I prepared to assess Hilary Clinton's acceptance speech. Her speech was delivered on July 28, 2016.

Here is what I submitted to the Los Angeles Times

Hilary Clinton acceptance speech

Thank you for the opportunity to offer some comments and observations on Hilary Clinton's speaking style. I watched her acceptance speech for the Democratic nomination on July 28, 2016. Hilary is a strong communicator and I offer these comments from my perspective.

Clinton's strength is her strong content and ideas which she communicates very well. At times she almost overwhelms with quantity and depth. The quality of her ideas and her experience are strengths which she illustrated well in her speech.

Her style is simple, direct and competent. Her voice is strong, her gestures are authoritative, and she makes solid eye contact with her audience.

She started very well by acknowledging the audience response and letting the audience enjoy their initial moments with her. She did an excellent job of meeting the audience's energy and enthusiasm. As she began, she quickly delved into personal areas such as her pride in her daughter and challenges that tested her and her husband. Later on, she continued by speaking of her grandfather's career at a mill, her mother's personal story, and her experiences in New Bedford, Massachussets and with Anastazia Samosa, Ryan Moore and Lauren Manning. These were good selections of personal stories that show a personal side to the audience. Audiences enjoy stories as they are memorable and usually relatable.

She used some very strong structure in the speech contrasting and characterizing her opponent's comments of 'I alone can fix it,' versus her 'we'll fix it together,' and 'none of us can fix it alone.' In this section of the speech she appealed to segments of her listeners by referencing teachers, doctors, police, entrepreneurs and mothers.

It's almost unfair that Obama has set the bar with style and humor. However, Hilary showed some self-deprecating humor when she said her opponent offers zero solutions and she 'loves talking about her plans' with a big smile. This plays well to her strength and the perception of being detail oriented and strong on policy.

A key message she landed was her statement that 'if fighting for child care is playing the woman card, then deal me in.' This was well paced and delivered and she allowed time for the audience to absorb the message.

Clinton's speech was strong in content and ideas. At times the quantity and depth of ideas was almost overwhelming. However, this does appear to be one of her strengths. The speech was well delivered, was clearly communicated and well received by her audience. It appeared that Clinton displayed her strengths well showing strong content and her more than competent style and technique.

Conclusion

The ideas I've shared are the result of study, practice, performance, and feedback received during 30 years of communicating with audiences of varying sizes and inclinations for a variety of organizations.

We live in a world where it is important for people to be able to state their points of view succinctly and accurately. This applies as employers, employees, family members, and citizens. Public speaking, and communication in general, are skills. Skills require study and practice.

I wish you success as you share your messages with broader audiences.

About Jim

Jim Kokocki is a keynote speaker, author, consultant and speech coach.

Jim serves as President and Board Chair of L'Arche Saint John, part of a worldwide network of communities creating homes, work, and day programs together with people who have intellectual disabilities.

Jim is a member of Toastmasters International and served as International President 2015-2016.

www.ingramcontent.com/pod-product-compliance
Lightning Source LLC
Chambersburg PA
CBHW020554220526
45463CB00006B/2306